An Arrow In My Quiver

an **ARROW** *in my quiver*
Raising my son with autism

Helen M. Koon

Dedication

This book is dedicated to parents of autistic children. I share your sacrificial love and persistence in helping your children to learn. May you find hope and encouragement in reading this book. May you find the treasures hidden inside each child that was given for a unique purpose.

> "Behold, children are a heritage from the Lord, the fruit of the womb is a reward. Like arrows in the hand of a warrior so are the children of one's youth. Happy is the man who has his quiver full of them! They shall not be shameful but shall speak with their enemies in the gate."
> (Psalm 127: 3-5)

Acknowledgment

I would like to thank my husband Derrick for partnering with me in raising Elliott. Because of the love we share in Christ, which allows us to look over each other's weaknesses, we are able to support each other in pursuing our destiny together.

I would like to thank our pastors at Convergence House of Prayer, Pastors Greg and Wendi Simas. They have cultivated a church community with intimacy and love for God, which helps Elliott to feel safe, accepted and loved. On June 26, 2011, Pastor Greg baptized Elliott, which brought great joy to the entire church body. Thanks also to, Pastor Gina Hyatt and Barbie Swihart with whom I could not do this book without. They pushed away other urgent matters and helped me with editing and formatting.

I would also like to thank the healing room ministry at Bethel Church in Redding, CA for praying for Elliott tirelessly over the years, bringing breakthrough, healing and encouragement to him. Without the ministry, we would not have been able to dream with God again.

Above all, I would like to thank Jesus for giving me a new life through His sacrifice on the cross. He gives me hope, healing and purpose in life. He is there for me in every situation and His love and faithfulness never fail. To Him be all the glory and honor, forever and ever.

Table Of Contents

Preface

I was born and raised in a well-to-do family in Hong Kong. My grandfather was a rich businessman and an entrepreneur. My father was a pilot and a boat builder. His boats were built for many prestigious clients around the world, especially in the United States. I was born to a Chinese Buddhist family that worshipped the ancestors, the Buddha, Qui Yen (the Queen of Mercy), the kitchen god, and almost anything.

My parents sent my siblings and me to either Christian or Catholic schools because those were more prestigious schools in Hong Kong in those days. It was by the grace of God that the seed of the gospel was sown early in our hearts.

At age 19, I became a Christian. It was not easy, as my parents treated me as if I had betrayed them. I was often persecuted. I would come home from a Christian gathering to find my bedding thrown out. My Bible and books were torn, dinner was withheld from me, and I would be sent to wash the family car, which was supposed to be the job of the servants. My parents deliberately made me bow before the ancestors' plaques on the 1st and 15th days of the month to test my faith and bullied me to conform. As much as I honored my ancestors, I could not worship them anymore. So I just stood there and prayed to God while holding back my emotion.

After finishing my education at Hong Kong Polytechnic in 1986, I worked as an occupational therapist in one of the outpatient rehabilitation centers helping hand injury patients to regain function after their injuries. It was a very rewarding and satisfying job, especially for a girl. My identity was my job. I was proud of my achievement and I was successful in my work.

In 1989, an opportunity came for me to immigrate to Canada. I was impressed with some of the knowledge and techniques that Canadian therapists demonstrated in treating patients and was hoping to further my training while working in Canada. I left home and started my new life in Waterloo, Ontario, Canada in 1990. I met my husband while in Toronto at a mutual friend's wedding in 1993 and we were married in 1994. Together we experienced the life changing power of God through the Holy Spirit in the Vineyard Church in Toronto (commonly called the Toronto Blessing) and through the sovereign move of the Holy Spirit, we were both set free from generational curses and emotional wounds related to our upbringing.

At that point we were ready to expand our family as we were both beyond our twenties. We had a house and good jobs. We traveled a bit and went on a few mission trips with our church, bringing the presence of God to people in Finland and Hawaii. With great longing and anticipation, and after having one miscarriage, Elliott Daniel Koon, our most precious son, was born on March 29, 1998. Little did we know Elliott's coming would forever change our lives.

Chapter 1

Miracle Birth In Canada

"It's positive, it's positive!" With overwhelming excitement, I woke up my husband to tell him the positive result of the pregnancy test. Yet on the other hand, I was hesitant due to the previous miscarriage and numerous months of disappointment. We had been trying to have a baby for over a year without success. I felt my biological clock was ticking, especially according to the Chinese standard. I believe a child is a gift from God. This baby was conceived after we went to a healing workshop in Orangeville, Ontario, Canada. During that time, many generational curses and inner vows were broken. We learned of and experienced God's love as a Father, which we had never experienced before.

With the excitement of the first sign of pregnancy, my mind started to dream about our future child. Would the baby be a boy or a girl? I didn't really mind if it was a girl or a boy despite the common Chinese preference. In my family, my dad treasured girls more than boys and I have three brothers and three sisters.

Over the next 9 months, my husband and I were talking and dreaming about our future child. We talked about possible names, both English and Chinese, and the types of sports the child could engage in.

We discussed what kind of character and upbringing we would want to cultivate in our child and whether we wanted to impart Chinese culture, or perhaps we should impart Canadian culture because we were living in Canada at the time. But since we both believed in Jesus and His resurrection power, we felt that the foundation of Christian living would be our choicest instruction in bringing up our child.

"Train up a child in the way he should go, and when he is old he will not depart from it." (Proverb 22:6)

The pregnancy was not all smooth and I felt vulnerable for the first time in my life, as I had no control over how the baby was developing inside of me. At 8 weeks, I started to have some spotting and the doctor put me on bed rest for a week. During that time, past memories of previous miscarriage haunted me. The many "what ifs" clouded my mind. Thankfully, the Holy Spirit reminded me that,

"For God has not given us a spirit of fear, but of power, and of love and of a sound mind." (II Timothy 1:7)

Our child was created by God, given to us as a gift. We are only temporary guardians. God is our child's ultimate Father and protector. So, I submitted the life of my unborn child to God and commanded the fear in me to leave. After one week of bed rest, I was fine and was allowed to return to work at the hospital as an occupational therapist.

After a month of working, I experienced a strong cramp followed by intense pain. I was afraid that the baby was in danger. Derrick and many in our church were praying for our unborn child. I felt helpless. Then the doctor ordered an ultrasound to see what was going on.

On the day of the ultrasound, Derrick was allowed to come into the room. For the first time, we both saw our baby's image and I knew he was going to be a boy (although the technician was not allowed to tell). The baby's feet resembled Derrick's. Every part of the baby was so tiny (he was only 3 months old) but he was so vibrant and lively, turning and kicking. In that moment, I appreciated life so much more. There was a tiny and beautiful creation of God living inside of me!!!! When Derrick called him and said "hello", he turned and waved back. It brought such joy to our hearts and especially to Derrick's. The ultrasound gave Derrick a new appreciation and excitement regarding fatherhood.

The ultrasound showed that I had a fibroid in my uterus that was causing the cramping and pain. The doctor couldn't do anything at that point and it had not caused any damage to the baby. Derrick kept praying for the baby, day and night, declaring healing to my womb and that the fibroid would dissolve on its own. Jesus, the Son of God, who was nailed on the cross for us bearing all pain and sickness, by the stripes He bore on the cross, He took away all our sin and sickness as well.

> *"But He was wounded for our transgressions, He was bruised for our iniquities; the chastisement for our peace was upon Him and by His stripes we are healed."* (Isaiah 53:5)

We could rightfully come to Jesus and ask for His healing of my womb. After those prayers, the pain and cramping didn't return throughout my pregnancy and the fibroid was not even detectable in subsequent ultrasounds. God had certainly answered our prayers and we couldn't thank Him enough.

During my pregnancy, I sang over our son and declared God's faithfulness and goodness, despite times of trouble. I wanted my son to hear and forever remember God's goodness. Instead of a lullaby, I sang to him the same song every night hoping that he felt peace and security in God's presence while in the womb. During that time, I continued to work at the hospital hoping to make it until the end of my pregnancy.

Since my mother lived with my sister an hour and a half away in Waterloo, Ontario, she was not able to come and help me throughout my pregnancy. In fact, she was still very angry with me for sharing the gospel of Jesus with my grandma (my dad's mom) four years prior. She thought that I caused grandma to betray the Buddha. She didn't know that Jesus was the only way to salvation. Calling another name or god except by calling on Jesus can save no one.

"And there is salvation in no one else, for there is no other name under Heaven given among men by which we must be saved." (Acts 4:12 ESV)

During my pregnancy, I did not have anyone to support me except God and my husband. Derrick's mom didn't live too far away from us (5 minutes by car and 30 minutes by walking), but she had difficulty walking long distance and was always anxious about everything. I didn't want to trouble her or cause her to worry about little things.

During the last trimester, I was resting a lot and was able to cook good, nutritious food for both Derrick and me by following a Chinese cookbook. I even had the postpartum cookbook ready. This was the most Chinese food I ever cooked in my life!!

At the last check up, the baby was almost one week overdue. My OBGYN said if the baby didn't come before that Sunday, I should check into the hospital anyway and that he would be on duty to induce me. My pastor's wife said to me, "your life will never be the same after the baby comes!" I didn't really understand what she meant since I had never been a mom, not to mention the mother of an autistic child!!

On the morning of March 29, 1998, Derrick and I went to the hospital. We were filled with anticipation and couldn't wait to meet our son and hold him in our arms. I checked in with the nurse and she immediately hooked me up with all the necessary tubes and the intravenous needle just in case I needed medication or if I ended up with a Caesarian. The baby's heartbeat was strong and fast, it almost sounded like a horse galloping. I asked the nurse if he was okay and she assured me that he was just fine.

As we waited for things to progress, there were no signs of stronger contractions. The doctor proceeded to break my water but still no further progression. I tried walking along the hallway, but after two hours there was still nothing happening. The doctor came again and suggested giving me "Oxytocin", which might bring on the contractions quicker, so we agreed.

Throughout my entire labor, Derrick was with me, pacing back and forth while praying for a safe delivery. He was praying the same Bible promises that he had been praying every night:

> *"Nevertheless, she will be saved in childbearing - if they continue in faith, love and holiness, with self-control."* (I Timothy 2:15)

Just a side note: Derrick wore a red shirt that day, a color of good luck (among Chinese) and celebration of the coming of the baby.

Fifteen minutes after the administration of the Oxytocin, I began to feel stronger and more frequent contractions. When it seemed unbearable, I found out I was 10cm dilated and it was time to push. I asked the Holy Spirit to help me to push through the pain. After just two pushes, and with the help of forceps, Elliott was born! It was a total miracle as to how fast and easy it was!

Elliott was beautiful and perfect! His fingers were so tiny and delicate. He was totally at peace, making a few noises here and there but he was completely at ease in my arms. Derrick adored him and he couldn't stop smiling. The nurses came to congratulate us. The whole birthing process was only about 40 minutes. It was such a miracle that God saved me from the prolonged labor pain that many women have. I felt truly blessed.

Derrick's mom came to visit and her eyes filled with tears when she met her first and only grandson. So we welcomed Elliott Daniel Koon into our world. He is named after the prophet Elijah which means, "my God is my Lord", and his middle name, Daniel, means, "my God is my judge". We also gave him a Chinese name: "官恩樂", which means grace and joy.

For the whole afternoon and evening we couldn't stop staring at Elliott. He was so peaceful and calm and his skin was so soft. The nurse gave Elliott his first bath. I was trying to learn everything from the nurse, such as how to bathe him properly, how to swaddle, and how to breastfeed effectively. I wanted to do everything perfectly.

No matter how much I wanted to keep Elliott with me the whole night, it was the hospital's policy to keep him in the nursery so that I could get my rest and sleep after giving birth. But I couldn't sleep very well. I walked to the nursery to see Elliott and peeked through the glass window making sure he was all right.

The night slipped away quickly. The doctor came to see me the next morning, checking on both Elliott and I. Since we were doing very well and there were no signs of distress, we were allowed to go home the next day.

With the car seat ready, Derrick came to take us home. We were so cautious about every little detail regarding our newborn son. Perhaps this was the sense of responsibility that came with parenthood. It was a new beginning for my life with a new role as a mother. My mother-in-law came to cook some of the traditional Chinese postpartum recipes to help my body recover from the trauma of the birthing process. Despite all of the special efforts she made, I couldn't really eat most of the food. Dishes like "ginger with pig feet", "herbal chicken soup", and "chicken and fungus" cooked in wine were totally repulsive to me or made my nose bleed. She was a bit disappointed as if her efforts were not appreciated, but I could only eat what went well with my body.

For the next month, I became a nursing machine keeping a round the clock supply of breast milk for Elliott. In the beginning, he didn't suck very well and I had to use a syringe to feed him every 2-3 hours. The amount of work was extraordinary and I could only take a nap when Elliott slept. He was so tiny and fragile that he could even fit on a floor cushion. As new parents, we also started to learn the meaning of his different cries so that we knew what he wanted when he cried. It was such a huge learning curve for both of us that I started to wonder why no one had ever warned us about the sacrifice one had to make before considering having a child. The job of parenthood is not for the faint hearted. Despite being an experienced occupational therapist with knowledge of human anatomy, physiology, psychology, I felt humbled learning parenting 101 and feeling totally unprepared.

During that time, a few of my family members from out of town came to visit us and to meet Elliott. They included my dear grandma who was in her 90's. She was so excited to meet her great grandson (4th generation). Some of my sisters and my brother-in-law also came, but my mother never came to visit. I called to tell her the news of Elliott's birth, but she didn't want to know or talk to me. I was glad that at least my grandma came.

When Elliott turned six weeks old, he began to cry non-stop from 6pm till midnight. No matter what we did (nursed him, walked him or rocked him), he would not stop crying. I read about how babies could get colic, but I refused to believe he was one of those. One night he was crying so hard that his skin felt warm and his cry sounded different from previous nights. So we felt we needed to take him to the hospital to make sure he was all right.

When we went to the hospital, the doctor ordered some blood tests and a chest x-Ray to make sure his lungs were clear and that he didn't have an infection or measles. Elliott continued to cry non-stop. It was very hard for me to see him crying to the point of shivering. Derrick was praying non-stop for Elliott and for God to heal him and bring peace to his body. He was praying for protection and binding up any fear, shock or trauma that was trying to enter Elliott's spirit at this young age. Upon X-Ray, his baby wrap was removed and the table was icy cold. I was told to hold his arms and legs out to expose the chest just like a turkey. It was so inhumane. Elliott couldn't stop crying and shivering and the technician was taking a long time to take the pictures. After the first one, she said it was not good enough since he moved. At that point I couldn't hold myself back anymore and I exclaimed, "No more pictures! That's enough!"

The technician said that the doctor would be upset if we didn't get a good picture. But I didn't care. I was his mother and believed they would not find anything in the X-Ray. The technician was reluctant to let us go, but she had no choice. This was the first time I saw the power of the protective nature inside this "mother hen"! I found myself having to defend my own son for the first time. Where was the timid and shy girl I once was?

After the whole ordeal was over, the doctor couldn't find anything. The bottom line was, "why was he crying like that?" I consulted the advice of other moms and read more books. I also asked for more prayers from friends in our church. At the least expected time, he just stopped crying at night suddenly. All I could say was that I stopped eating broccoli and I changed the way I breast fed him and prayed a lot. But little did we know that his digestive system probably was very sensitive.

As his crying settled down, I thought I could enjoy some quiet and a normal life as a mom. I thought I would simply watch Elliott grow through all the developmental milestones just as I had dreamed of. But then one night Derrick said he would like to move to the Silicon Valley in California where all the visionaries in computer software are.

I was surprised, though this was not the first time he had brought this up. I remembered that one year after we were married, Derrick expressed the idea of moving as he felt that the computer companies in Canada were very conservative in adopting cutting-edge technologies. But why now? The timing was not quite right. Elliott was just born and I was still recovering. I took the whole issue to the Lord and asked if it was the right time or the right thing to do. Since the Bible promises said,

> "My sheep hear my voice and I know them, and they follow me," (John 10:27)

I trusted God to direct our path, especially in a major decision like moving to a different country. To my surprise, I felt so much peace about it as I asked God about the move. So I agreed.

If it was in Derrick's heart to do so, I believed it was best to do it while we were young. If we liked it there, we would stay. If not, we could move back in two years. However, I wanted to go to Silicon Valley to check it out first before making a final decision.

We left for San Francisco at the end of July 1998 when Elliott was four months old. We spent one month living in a hotel in Sunnyvale, CA to see if Derrick would receive an interesting job offer.

After we spent a month in Sunnyvale, Derrick had a job offer. So we returned to Toronto to arrange the details of the move. We put our house up for sale, as we didn't know how long we would stay in the USA. We sold our house within the first day of our open house. We both resigned from our jobs. The hardest thing to do was to say goodbye to our church friends and to our families, especially Derrick's mom and my grandma. But just as we left Hong Kong in the late 80's, I had so much peace about going to California knowing that God would be with us wherever we went. Little did we know that God had already prepared our path and destiny in California! If we were still in Canada, we would probably be financially bankrupt due to Elliott's needs.

Chapter 2

Moving To California

Everything happened so rapidly. We came to Foster City, California (30 minutes drive from downtown San Francisco) with two suitcases and a six month old baby. With the fascinating plan of God, He prepared an apartment for us through a high school girlfriend that lived in the same city. The apartment was half the size of our townhouse in Canada, but we thought we would only stay there temporarily. The apartment had a beautiful lagoon view and a walkway along the lagoon. It was perfect for a new family.

So here we were, alone in a new country. We had no family except Derrick's 90-year-old grandma who lived with his uncle in San Francisco. I had two high school friends that were within 30 minutes driving distance from us. But I had no car and they both had their school-aged children to take care of. It was very hard to expect them to come and help me. Derrick was required to start work the day after we arrived. I was left to figure out the rest: a new apartment, no friends, a new city and a new country. All our social ties were broken off as we moved so far away from our church friends and families in Canada. Where should I begin? As a new mom, what were the do's and don'ts of raising a healthy baby?

I was a bit lonely and felt a bit helpless. All I could do was pray to God, asking for wisdom and discernment as to what to do in different situations. He promises to help.

> *"If any of you lacks wisdom, let him ask God, who gives to all liberally and without reproach, and it will be given to him." (James 1:5)*

Besides the Bible, there were two books I brought from Canada that had been instrumental in educating me about parenting. The first one was "What To Expect The First Year" by Heidi Murkoff[1]. This book gave me month-to-month information about newborns as well as what were signs of abnormality so that I could check with the doctor. The other book was "The Complete Book Of Christian Parenting And Child Care" by Dr. William Sears[2]. In his book, I learned about attachment parenting.

> *"Attachment parenting focuses on the nurturing connection that parents can develop with their children. This nurturing connection is viewed as the ideal way to raise secure, independent and empathetic children. Proponents of this parenting philosophy, including Dr.Sears, believed a secure, trusting attachment to parents during childhood*

forms the basis for secure relationships and independence as adult."[3]

With my background as a therapist and my knowledge in human psychology and psychiatry, I knew that feeling secure was very important in order for a person to develop confidence. Without security and confidence, one can have problems in developing relationships with others. It can even affect one from exploring and finding one's calling, and the list is just endless.

Through the healing workshops in Orangeville, Ontario Canada, I came to understand that the role of godly parents is to provide love, provision, protection, teaching, correction and discipline to their children. Godly parents also demonstrate faithfulness, show physical affection and spend time with their children, as well as setting a godly example because parents are supposed to be the representation of how God loves us, since He made us in *His* image.

> *"Then God said 'Let Us make man in Our image, according to Our likeness, let them have dominion over the fish of the sea...."*. (Genesis 1:26)

So we bear His character of love, kindness, gentleness, faithfulness and compassion. God loves us perfectly and unconditionally. The Son of God (Jesus) loves us and gave Himself for us on the cross even before we knew Him.

> *"For God so loved the world, that He gave His only begotten son, that whoever believes in Him*

should not perish but have everlasting life." (John 3:16)

God doesn't love us for what we do for Him. We cannot earn or buy His love. He loves us unconditionally because that is His nature. He is the God of love.

This concept of God's love was very different from what I experienced growing up in a Chinese family. I grew up being told I was ugly, dumb and naughty by my parents and grandma all the time, even though I was very gentle, kind, softhearted, obedient and most conscientious. Chinese parenting concepts believe that if parents praise their children for being good or looking pretty, they will become too proud of themselves and they would behave like a brat. Humility is highly valued in Asian culture. Yet false humility, as I would say, would turn one into a hypocrite. So under this kind of upbringing, I felt everyone, including my parents and teachers, were rejecting me. How would I expect other people to like me? Children were not allowed to speak for themselves or express their opinion. I was suppressed and did not have a good self-image. I tried to please my parents so badly in order to earn their favor and love. I would get my dad's slippers ready and wait for him to come home, offering them to him in exchange for a "good job, well done my daughter" or a pat on my head, or to be called "good girl". But those words never came. I also studied hard to get good grades so that my parents would be proud of me. Again, I felt like I was never good enough.

Eventually I realized that the ways my parents expressed love was by providing us with a good home and all the basic essentials like food and clothing. But their love language was different from mine. What I longed for was their love and affirmation. I didn't receive it. If I didn't "perform" according to their expectations, I would be spanked brutally. How could I feel safe or valued by my closest family?

Having gone through what I did, I made a decision to love Elliott the best I could by following God's instructions. I would give him unconditional love and attend to his every cry and needs. I wanted to be there for him always. My hope was that by providing him with security and stability through attachment parenting, I would be able to give him a good start and he wouldn't feel rejected by his own parents like I did.

Sure enough, Elliott liked my approach very much. I carried him in a sling and maintained constant interaction with him. I held him and looked him in his eyes. When he cooed, I cooed back. We were very happy together. Even when I needed to move around, did housework, cooked or went shopping, he was always with me in the sling. There was no separation anxiety and he was very secure and happy. I was off to a great start in my childrearing experience.

We traveled a lot back and forth to Canada whenever Derrick changed his job. Surprisingly, it was not a problem for Elliott as he was secure in the sling as we traveled from place to place. The only little problem I noticed was that he seemed to cry a lot more while I was trying to pack. He would cry so hard that his face would turn red and he would look feverish. Even the cleaning lady in the hotel thought he was sick. We didn't know at that time that he was just super sensitive to a lot of things. Perhaps the cry was due to the notion of changes as he saw me packing and didn't like the change.

At that time we didn't notice any problems in Elliott's development, except that he wasn't crawling at six months and had skipped right to cruising between furniture. I thought this was fine, since I knew that all children grow at their own pace and timing. I was not fixated on all the details of the developmental milestones, even though I am a therapist and aware of the different stages and timing for development.

I spent all of my time at home with Elliott while Derrick worked long hours at his computer job, which required him to travel an hour each way to work. I enjoyed spending time with Elliott while taking him to the park and listening to stories at the library. I would read to him and take him to baby gymnastics classes at the recreational center to facilitate his gross motor development. My most favorite outing was to take him to toy stores. I would use my knowledge in activities analysis to select toys that had the most developmental value for Elliott. I found so many fun toys that I didn't grow up with. The child in me came alive. I literally wanted to buy everything for him that was good for his sensory, motor, cognitive, emotional and perceptual development. You could have called me a tiger mom too as I watched over him intensely. I wanted him to do well and to be smarter than other kids. Ironically, it was Elliott who told me to put the toys back as he didn't want them. Otherwise my house would have no room to walk around!

Just like many parents, we were elated with every little new move Elliott made. His first step and first words of "dad" and "mom" made us feel so excited. We celebrated his first birthday, and he started to walk at 16 months. One afternoon, as I went to pick him up from his afternoon nap, I heard him say, "Mom, I am a worshiper."

I wasn't sure what I heard since he was not talking in sentences yet. He was only able to say a few single words like "yes", "no", "mom", or "dad". I was surprised but yet I immediately recognized that it was the Holy Spirit uttering to me about Elliott's calling and He was giving me guidance in terms of how I should nurture him for his destiny.

From then on, whenever we could, we would bring Elliott to churches where there were worship music and a strong presence of God. I believed God could minister to him and communicate to Elliott in a way that is beyond what language can express.

Things were going very well, or so I thought. But at his second year wellness check up, the pediatrician told us that Elliott's language development was a bit behind and she recommended him undergo a speech evaluation. I thought Elliott was just slow in speech because he was a boy, as girls develop language much sooner. Besides, we spoke both English and Cantonese at home, so it might just take a little while for him to get a good grip of both languages. The doctor wanted us to speak to him only in English so that he would not be confused. I said to the doctor, "I believe he will improve. It is just a matter of time". In my mind, I thought he was just fine. At least he was not lining up cars, spinning or flapping his hands, which I learned from my therapy training as classic symptoms of autism. But I didn't know that he was not off the hook yet.

Chapter 3

The Honeymoon Was Over

One morning in April of 2000, while I was keeping my eyes and ears open for Elliott's language to further develop, I received a phone call from my endocrinologist. Earlier that week, I was at his office undergoing a needle biopsy of a lump in my neck that had been there for over two or three years which I hadn't been paying attention to. The phone call was unsettling.

The biopsy showed that there were some cancerous tissues in the lump. The doctor suggested I come in for another biopsy and possible surgery to remove the lump. I was in disbelief. This had to be a mistake, since I had no symptoms. I agreed to the second biopsy. The doctor stated that because the cancer was in the thyroid gland, there would be no symptoms. He said it was a very slow growing cancer and possibly the best cancer one could get because the recovery rate was very high. The doctor strongly suggested I have it removed. In my mind I knew God could heal me; there was no doubt about it.

> *"...for I am The Lord who heals you."* (Exodus 15:26)

It was a promise from His Word. Elliott was only two years old. The thought of having to have surgery and being separated from Elliott disturbed me. I would not be able to continue breastfeeding and I would have to wean him immediately. My child development class taught me that age two is the time when children develop object constancy. If the secure person in his life suddenly disappears, it would create a long-term effect of insecurity and loss. I had spent so much time fostering security through attachment parenting in order to avoid insecurity in Elliott, how could I give it up so easily? I felt I had no choice but to avoid the surgery and depend on God's healing.

The doctor subsequently did another biopsy, which turned out to be negative, but he was not entertained by my testimony of God's faithfulness and he still insisted that I schedule the surgery. He also asked the nuclear medicine doctor to call me to describe the necessary treatment after the surgery hoping to convince me to proceed. I turned them all down but weaned Elliott just in case I had to do something drastic. Elliott cried intensely and I could only hold my tears back as I "denied" him his source of comfort.

Meanwhile, Derrick was worried about me. He brought me to every healing conference near and far to receive prayer, including Argentina in 2000, where there was a healing revival taking place. He didn't want me to die nor did he want Elliott to grow up without a mother. I was fully aware of that, but I believed God could heal me. It was just a matter of time. We read many books on God's healing and recited His promises from the Bible to encourage ourselves. I did not plan to die, and I had not given up at all, even though there was no physical sign of change in the lump after all of the prayers. One of the scriptures I held onto was:

> *"I shall not die, but live, and declare the works of the Lord."* (Psalm 118:17)

I wanted to trust God for my healing, but at times I was impatient. During those times, I focused more on the care of Elliott, watching him grow and celebrating every moment we had together. I tried to keep some normalcy at home and avoided entertaining the "what ifs". I wanted to see Elliott grow up and celebrate every milestone of his development.

We celebrated his second and third birthdays without many noticeable problems except that his speech was still delayed compared to his peers. I continued to play with him at home, and take him to the park, but he didn't seem to enjoy it as other children did. He wouldn't play in the sand and he couldn't really ride a tricycle. He was having difficulty climbing stairs and he avoided going down the slide unless I put him on my lap and went down together. Children normally play for hours at the park, but he always wanted to go home and had no interest in playing with other children. He was only interested in interacting with his parents. I thought it might be because he didn't have enough kids around him to play with. But despite joining playgroups and classes at the recreational center or setting up play dates with other kids, he didn't show much interest in them at all.

At 3 ½ years old, I had to take Elliott to the dentist for the first time. He was scared of the dentist and barely opened his mouth for the check up. The dentist said he had a lot of cavities due to prolonged breastfeeding and suggested fillings. He wanted to split the work into three half-hour sessions. I trusted the dentist because a friend's child went to him as well.

They had given me some medication that would calm Elliott prior to the appointment. Once we arrived, the nurse took him in without me. I was told it would be better if Elliott did not see me so that the dentist could do his job. As soon as Elliott went in, I heard him crying. My heart was filled with pain as well because I had never left him with anyone besides Derrick, especially for a doctor's appointment. He continued to cry helplessly and my heart sank. I didn't know what exactly was happening behind the door. Since I was not allowed to go in to help comfort him during the procedure, the only thing I could do was to pray for God's protection and comfort. This continued for half an hour. By the time the procedure was done, Elliott was exhausted from crying and I was too. He was crying non-stop even though I held him in my arms. I felt so bad for him, yet I knew it was necessary to keep his teeth healthy. But I didn't know what he went through in the dentist chair.

He finally completed all three dental appointments with caps and fillings being put on the teeth. Every time Elliott was there, he cried through the whole half-hour appointment and I did too. It was four years later that I realized the dentist was using a strap to hold him down for the ordeal, which had traumatized him at 3.5 years old. It probably caused the fear of separation and fear for any new experiences.

This might explain why he had such a difficult time starting pre-school in the fall right after the dental appointments in the summer.

Just like all parents, we wanted to give Elliott a good start at school. We looked around and I chose the best pre-school in our area. We went to the open house and chatted with the principal and teachers. We felt it would be a great school for him as the teachers were so loving and kind.

Right after Labor Day 2001, I dropped him off at his first day of preschool. It should have been a fun and exciting time, as he would meet and play with new friends. On the contrary, he started crying as soon as I left him at school. I read about separation anxiety with children starting school. But why Elliott? I had always been careful not to allow insecurity and fear to develop in him by practicing attachment parenting and I was always there for him. Hadn't he already developed a sense of trust that would allow him to feel secure and to venture out to do something new, especially something fun like school?

Unfortunately, the crying continued for the entire first week of preschool (3.5 hours per day). I sat outside the school every day waiting just in case the teacher wanted me to help or to take him home. But they didn't call me. Eventually the crying only lasted for an hour a day and I thought he was finally getting used to school.

To my surprise, just before Christmas, the teacher said she wanted to meet with me after school. The principal was also there. They described to me how difficult it was for Elliott to attend class, to do art, or listen to stories. They said he would run outside even if they blocked the exit. They said he would play with the water fountain and light switches. They had a hard time keeping him under control and so the preschool couldn't take care of him anymore. They told me to look for another school.

This came as a shock to me, especially as this was just before Christmas. I was sure the school didn't take their decision lightly, but how would I explain to Elliott that he could not go to that school anymore? We didn't see this coming at all and we didn't have an alternate plan in place. I was in shock and disappointed. I felt rejected. I wanted to beg and plead for them to keep Elliott, but I knew they had already made up their minds.

So during the Christmas holiday, I frantically looked for another preschool close enough to our house. Thankfully, we found one! With renewed hope, I brought him in the first day and prayed that he wouldn't cry like before. He was fine and there was no complaint, at least for the first week. But my hopes were soon dashed.

After the first month in the second preschool, the principal called me in. She was very straight forward with me and said she suspected that Elliott had some problems as he couldn't settle down to participate in class and he wasn't able to follow instructions. She suggested I take him to the doctor for a formal evaluation. She gave me a list of resources and said she would refund the school fees, as I would need the money to help him.

Here I was, the second time round, feeling shocked and rejected again! How could this be? What was going on? Why would they tell me that there was something wrong with Elliott yet he was able to communicate with me well at home? I didn't know what to do. He needed to go to school to learn and I had no experience in home schooling and didn't know the American school system well enough to teach him.

Upon leaving the meeting at the preschool, my mind went blank and my heart sank deeper than before. Again I had to search for another preschool quickly so that he wouldn't miss any time in learning. I made an appointment with our pediatrician and told her the problems we encountered in school. I also requested a formal evaluation to attempt to figure out what was going on with Elliott. Physically, he seemed to be a normal four year old. But he still couldn't jump and he was not able to form complete sentences yet.

Another strange thing was that he continued to be very clingy especially when we went to new places or saw new people. When we were with friends or in social gatherings where people laughed suddenly, he would be startled and cry. Of course that caused a bit of embarrassment and some even gave us a dirty look. But what could I do? There must be something that was bothering him but we couldn't figure out the cause.

I started to read books and tried to find some answers. I started wondering if he had some sort of an attention deficit or sensory motor disorder. But the self-diagnosis and guessing here and there didn't help at all because it caused more worry and stress. Since I had no experience as a mom, and I didn't have a lot of close friends that I could share my heart with, I felt lonely and helpless. Where could I find the help he needed?

I took him to the speech therapist for an evaluation. He was also referred to the developmental psychologist to find out what was causing all the problems in school. As I sat in the waiting room, I was prepared for the worst but hoping for the best.

When the developmental psychologist came out to talk to me after the evaluation, he said Elliott was very warm and was able to follow simple instruction. There was no hand flapping or lining up toys or ritualistic movement. When he said that, I realized that he was trying to see if Elliott was autistic.

In my training as an occupational therapist, I came across the diagnosis of autism. Usually children are diagnosed by the age of two if they have difficulty with speech and in interacting with their environment. It is often difficult for them to interact with others (both adults and children), as they hide themselves in their own world and many have a lot of behavioral problems. They might spin around and have difficulty tending to tasks. I was relieved when Elliott turned two and he didn't have the typical symptoms of autism. However, he did have delay in speech and gross motor development. Yet at the time, I didn't know autism was being redefined as a spectrum with a variety of levels of functions and disabilities.

When the report from the developmental psychologist came, I was somewhat relieved with the diagnosis of "multiple developmental delay, including speech, fine and gross motor delay." This would explain why the regular preschool couldn't handle him, as they didn't have the resources to teach special needs children.

At that time, I didn't know of any special education preschool. My only choice was to call the school district in our city to have him assessed. In California, if a child has special needs and is under three years of age, the regional center would be responsible for their care and education. However, if the child is over three years of age, it is the responsibility of the school district to educate him. Elliott was then assessed by the school psychologist and speech therapist and they came to the conclusion that Elliott had multiple areas of delay and they would have him start the special needs school in October, 2003. No diagnosis of autism was given.

At a barbecue picnic just before school started, I met the teachers and many parents of special needs children that were attending the same school. One thing I found in common was that they were all very friendly and seemed to have a lot of love and acceptance for children with special needs. Elliott was my only child and I loved him dearly. However, I knew that if I were in Hong Kong, or if I were close to my own Chinese cultural environment, they would not understand or accept him because of his special needs. There is a stigma associated with any form of disability. This was a hard reality. I was shocked to find out that my son was not welcomed even in some of my social circles. This was a very difficult fact to swallow.

I felt rejected by some of my Chinese friends. Elliott was so young and innocent and he didn't choose to have autism. He was being rejected by my friends for something he could not control. Oh, how cruel this reality was! But then I remembered that I could choose to be angry at them, or I could choose to forgive them and move on.

What I needed at that time was a loving and supportive environment for Elliott to grow up in. Although some would reject him, our Father in heaven loved him. That was most reassuring. Besides, both Derrick and I loved him. If I didn't love and accept Elliott, who would? If I didn't believe in his potential, then who would? I was reminded that Elliott was beautifully and wonderfully made by God:

> *"For you formed my inward parts, you covered me in my mother's womb. I will praise you for I am fearfully and wonderfully made."* (Psalm 139:13-14)

I believed God had a plan and purpose for him on earth. God made him perfect and loves him no matter what. Therefore, I decided to choose carefully whom I would spend my time with. I needed support in bringing up Elliott but I couldn't handle negative people around me, or those that would pass judgment on us. Elliott was very sensitive to his environment. Somehow he could sense even a negative tone of voice or negative vibes from people around him.

At that time, I had already reconciled with my mother in Canada but I couldn't explain to her about our difficulties with Elliott because she would compare Elliott to his two other cousins. Thankfully, Derrick's mom was completely supportive and was always eager to hear our stories whenever we called her long distance.

Although I didn't know what the future held and how Elliott's new school experience would be, the only thing I could do was to take it one step at a time and trust that God would be with us on the journey.

Chapter 4

I Was Not Alone

The morning finally came when the yellow school bus from the public school came to pick Elliott up for his first day of pre-kindergarten. I was very thankful for this new beginning. I met the teacher at the school barbecue and found her very knowledgeable and kind. She had two teaching aides in her class to help out. The class was very small, only six children. There were 5 boys and 1 girl and they all had problems with speech and language development. Some could not talk or focus at all, and others could only utter one or two words. The class was four hours a day, five days a week. The classroom was very structured. Every morning the same routine was followed as the teachers tried to get the children to focus and be attentive, as well as to follow simple instructions, which were fundamental for learning.

At that time, I was still a stay-at-home mom since we came to California on Derrick's work visa. I had a dependent visa that didn't allow me to work. I was relieved that Elliott was finally getting some help at this special needs school. Occasionally I would go to the school playground to peek and to make sure Elliott was doing alright. I would often see the aides or the teacher trying to encourage Elliott to participate in playground play. They tried to get him to try out the tricycle, but he was not interested. After a few months, I still didn't hear feedback from the teacher. I guess no news was good news, as that might mean the school was able to help him and he was settling in well. I waited for him to arrive home in the yellow bus every day. He usually looked tired and was not able to tell me what he did at school or whether he liked school or not. His expressive language was still very limited, though I suspected that he understood more than I thought he could.

At the school open house, we met the teacher and others parents from the class. The teacher introduced the parents to each other, and she wanted to set up a monthly parent support group so that we could support each other and share our experiences. At that time, I realized that all of the children in the class had been diagnosed with autism except Elliott. Somehow our doctor didn't give him that diagnosis. Maybe there was still a lot of uncertainty and hesitation among doctors to label children with autism due to the stigma that was associated with it.

Through the parent teacher support group, the teacher, speech therapist and occupational therapist explained in more detail how the class was structured in order to facilitate the development of the children. I was very glad that God led us to California through Derrick's work, as I knew we would not see this kind of understanding, acceptance or resources available to us even in Canada, and of course not in Hong Kong.

Since Elliott was diagnosed with multiple delays, he was not able to get the many resources available from the school or our insurance company, such as speech therapy or ABA (Applied Behavior Analysis - an approach to teach children with autism that has been proven to be effective). Despite the challenges in his speech and language development, as well as fine and gross motor skills development, the medical insurance didn't provide any services for treatment except physical therapy once a week for four visits. Even with that, I had to make multiple phone calls to advocate for Elliott and justify the need for therapy.

Deep in my mind, I knew he would also need speech therapy and occupational therapy, especially for sensory processing and integration. I knew these therapies could help him to decrease his hypersensitivity to sound and touch. But the only way he could get these therapies was through the school district unless I paid for them privately. The cost of therapy was extremely expensive, especially since he would require many weeks, months or even years of therapy. But what could I do? Everyone says that the first five years of a child's development is most important. The earlier the intervention, the better the results would be. So I had no choice but to pay out of pocket for the weekly occupational therapy to help with Elliott's sensory motor development.

At that time, the school district was piloting an afternoon program with the speech and occupational therapist two days per week to help with speech and gross motor development through play. I was very thankful to have all of the extra help for Elliott.

The school year went by fast, but I still didn't see much improvement with Elliott's language. At five and a half years, he still continued to have no interest in playing with other children. He could only speak one to two word sentences, and he didn't know how to read. He was very clingy and wanted me to carry him all the time, especially while in a new environment.

We were attending a church service on a Sunday in San Francisco and he joined the children in Sunday school. The teachers were very kind to him, but he had difficulty in following instructions most of the time and required one-on-one assistance in order to keep him in the program. When the class didn't have enough helpers, he would sit with us. This could be a problem as well, since he would make noises while the speaker was talking. At times it would be quite loud and distracting to others who were trying to listen to the sermon. Some church members were kind enough to ignore the noises and tried to stay focus. But for others who didn't understand, they would give us strange looks, indicating that we should bring him outside. That certainly put a lot of pressure on us, just like the experience with my Chinese friends, which could be hurtful at times.

Socially, we came across many situations that were embarrassing, especially when we went to restaurants. Derrick likes to eat out, especially Japanese food, but most of the restaurant atmospheres are very quiet. Elliott struggled to stay in the high chair, or he would walk around the restaurant disturbing other customers. We had to take turns following him or entertaining him so that he would stay seated. There was really not much time for us to enjoy the food and the ambience. Because it was not an enjoyable experience, we ended up not going out much at all.

At the end of the first school year, the teacher decided to come for a home visit. I never had a teacher come for a home visit in Hong Kong or in Canada. Perhaps if someone were in trouble it would warrant a social worker coming for a home visit. My fear was that she might tell me that something was wrong with Elliott. Or perhaps she would tell me that he was not able to fit in just like the other schools had said.

The teacher arrived with the occupational therapist that day. After a warm conversation about how Elliott was currently doing at school, the teacher asked why Elliott hadn't received an autism diagnosis. I didn't know why I was being asked that. Did Elliott look like he had autism? Was he having more trouble than I thought? My response to her question was that the doctor had only given us a diagnosis of multiple delays.

The teacher went on to explain that Elliott had many areas of difficulty, including language delay, gross and fine motor delay. He also had difficulty in relating to his peers, which were all diagnostic criteria for autism. She said it would be better for him to have

49

the appropriate diagnosis so that he could qualify for the services designated to autistic children.

So I met with the school district and the IEP team (Individual Education Plan). The school psychologist suggested that I take Elliott to an autism specialist within our insurance network so that he could be given a proper diagnosis.

At that time in 2004, autism cases started to increase in the Bay Area as well as rapidly around the world. The ratio of children with autism was 1 in 160 (the ratio is currently 1 in 68). However, schools and medical providers were not ready to deal with the sudden increase of cases, and they didn't have much of a formalized process to make appropriate diagnoses. Many families, like us, would fall through the cracks and not receive early intervention. I heard some people recommend that children with autism should have early intervention, including 40 hours per week of ABA in order to help them to learn effectively. Of course without a formal diagnosis of autism, Elliott was not able to get the resources he needed from the school district. I didn't mind the diagnosis or the label, but the doctor hadn't given the diagnosis to Elliott. I felt the urgency to push for a proper diagnosis.

So I brought Elliott to see the autism specialist. I had mixed feelings, as I really wanted him to get the services that would help him to develop, as he was almost six years old. I was also hoping that she would tell me that Elliott didn't have autism, so I could feel relieved.

I patiently waited with Elliott, although I was a bit nervous. The specialist finally arrived and began asking why I came to see her. I told her about Elliott's situation. She asked him what his name was. Before Elliott could respond, she began telling me about her own son, and I finally felt there was someone who understood my struggle.

Her son had high functioning autism and was a freshman at UC Irvine in Southern California. She told me how she located an educational consultant to help him to find his niche but that it was costing her a lot of money. She talked non-stop about her son for 45 minutes. Her conclusion was that Elliott had moderate autism along with gross motor and language delay. I was relatively calm when I heard the diagnosis, as all I wanted were answers so that Elliott could receive the services and help he needed. I wanted to make sure that she would write a prescription for 40 hours of weekly ABA services, as well as occupational and speech therapy, so that the school district would provide these services to Elliott.

While sitting in a local bookstore after the doctor appointment, a million thoughts flooded my mind. I really wasn't sure how I should feel about the diagnosis. Should I be happy that I finally got the prescription for services for Elliott? What did it mean to have a diagnosis of autism? What would his future be like? I told my friends that I didn't mind the label. Did I really feel that way? Or would it mean that his future has come to a halt? Isn't it every parent's dream to see his/her child grow up healthy and happy, going to school and college and then finding a job, a spouse and starting his/her own family? Having the label of autism made it appear that these dreams for our Elliott would be forever shattered. Would he be able to live independently after we pass on? Would he be forever rejected by society, especially the Asian community? Would my friends and family see him as an outcast? All of these thoughts were flooding my mind and it felt like my world had suddenly stopped. I was confused and discouraged. What about the prophetic words that I had received in Toronto in 1995 that I would be "going to the nations and healing the sick and setting the captives free?" What about the "yes" that I said to God during a mission trip to Argentina that I would go and set the prisoners of the heart free? How could I accomplish my calling with Elliott's diagnosis of autism on top of the thyroid cancer in my body? The diagnosis was like a death sentence that weighed heavily on my heart. I found myself sitting on the bench with tears dripping down my face. At that moment, my world seemed to freeze. I didn't care who was looking at me.

I started to flip through a book in my hand called, "You Will Dream New Dreams -- Inspiring Stories By Parents Of Children With_Disabilities" (Klein and Schive)[4]. This book is a collection of stories written by parents with children of different kinds of disabilities, including Down Syndrome and Attention Deficit Disorder. As I read the first sentence in the foreword, it said, "You are not alone". Tears were running down my face, and I felt a warm embrace from Heaven through this book. It was as if God wanted to remind me that I was not alone on this journey. He was there for me and with me, just like the Bible said in Hebrews 12:1-2:

> *"Therefore, we also, since we are surrounded by so great a cloud of witnesses, let us easily lay aside every weight, and the sin which so easily ensnares us, and let us run with endurance the race that is set before us, looking to Jesus, the author and finisher of our faith, who for the joy that was set before him endured the cross, despising the shame, and has sat down at the right hand of the throne of God."*

Yes, Jesus is the author and finisher of our faith. He is the one I could count on when I don't know what to do. He is the one who gives me the faith to go on even though the next step was not completely clear. I could only take one step at a time as the battle for Elliott had just begun.

Chapter 5

A Glimmer Of Hope

It was March 2004 and Elliott just turned six years old. I received the final report from the autism specialist. She gave him a diagnosis of autism and recommended 20 hours of ABA services per week to help his social and emotional development. I then called an IEP meeting with the school district and requested these services along with the special education class and speech therapy. However, since ABA services are an intensive one-on-one therapy, it would cost the school district thousands of dollars per month to provide them. In order to avoid the huge expenses, the school psychologist offered additional speech therapy outside of the school setting to help settle my concerns about Elliott's language delay. I happily accepted the extra speech therapy offered to help Elliott's language development. Even so, I continued to exert the need for

ABA services through the school district as recommended by Elliott's doctor.

After a long wait and lots of prayers, the Director of Special Education finally called me at work one afternoon and offered the ABA services. I literally jumped up and down and announced the great news to all of my colleagues as if it was the best day of my life.

It was by God's grace for Elliott that the director was so generous in the offer. Along with the 13 hours a week of one-on-one ABA home services that would help Elliott develop pre-learning skills for school, he would also have an aide trained in ABA to facilitate learning in a regular kindergarten classroom. I insisted that Elliott attend a regular classroom in the fall in order to get more social exposure and language modeling, which had not been available in his special education class the previous two years.

At that time, Elliott was only able to express himself using 3-4 word sentences, but mostly he preferred using just 1-2 words at a time. He wasn't able to sit in the teaching circle, as he wanted to get up every 1-2 minutes to walk around. He wasn't able to sit still for non-preferred tasks. He didn't have any interest in other school children and he always kept to himself at lunch or break times. He was easily overwhelmed by the noises on the playground. Though he might appear to be smiling, his mind probably was somewhere else. I was grateful that the ABA services were starting and I was hopeful that this would change everything.

That April, my doctor finally caught up with me as I was avoiding the issue of my own health. She asked whether I wanted to see my son grow up, referring to the fact that I still had a cancerous lump in my thyroid. She said I should take care of myself rather than just looking after my child with autism.

At that time, the stress of my own health issues and the need to secure the best services for Elliott was getting to me. I was tired. I often found myself in tears while running around from school to home and to different therapy sessions. The stress was astronomical. I became very discouraged, sad, and full of despair. The overwhelming sense of an unknown future, the reality of Elliott's disability, the frustration and loneliness, the isolation from family in Canada, the rejections from friends, the limitation in my own physical health, just to name a few things, had gotten to me. Now there was an additional load on my plate, a surgery to remove my thyroid cancer! I asked God why. Why me? I didn't choose this path nor did I have a choice. There were so many unknowns, yet I needed to gather my emotional strength and be strong for Elliott and for my husband. Derrick was also confronted with a benign but fast-growing tumor on the left side of his face near the salivary gland and that was affecting his hearing. He was not sure what to do, especially with the affliction that was happening around him.

One day, I met with my pastor's wife at church in San Francisco. She wanted to know how I felt about the final diagnosis for Elliott and to make sure I was okay. I told her about all of the despair I had been feeling and the questions I had. She invited me to pray with her, as we asked God for His perspective about my situation and about Elliott's diagnosis, despite of what the doctor said.

As I closed my eyes to focus on connecting with God, I saw a picture of Elliott. He was a grown up, wearing a grey colored suit and was speaking eloquently in front of a huge crowd of people. I didn't know whether he was teaching or preaching. Then I saw a yellow balloon with a happy face falling down from above as if it was a sign of goodness, happiness and joy.

As I shared this picture with my pastor's wife, tears welled up in my eyes. I knew this was from God. He encouraged me by giving me a glimpse of Elliott 's future destiny so that I would not lose hope. He is a good God and a good Father in Heaven. In the Bible it says,

> "where there is no prophetic vision, the people cast off restraint, but blessed is he who keeps the law" (Proverb 29:18 ESV).

My dreams for Elliott died a few weeks earlier when I first received the autism diagnosis. But by the grace of God, He gave me a vision so that I could have hope.

With that picture in my mind, God had given me direction on how to pray for Elliott. I started to pray for his language abilities, as he was destined to speak, not only to people around him, but also to a big audience.

Remembering what I learned, that words have power, I knew we could choose to say words of blessing or words that curse. . I started to declare the integration of the left and right brain. I declared healing in the information processing area of the brain, as well as the coordination of gross and fine motor areas in the brain. Many Chinese parents are instructed to say negative words about their children in order to prevent them from being arrogant. Instead of affirming their children, they, unaware, speak curses over their children. The words I spoke over Elliott would make a big difference in how he grew up. I decided to partner with God for Elliott's destiny as He gave me a glimpse of new hope through the picture.

Because of that glimpse of hope, I went through my thyroid surgery. While I was in the hospital, Elliott experienced his first time being away from me. Derrick was able to take care of Elliott by himself including the changing of diapers. Yes, Elliott was still wearing diapers at six years old because he was not able to control his bowel movements. Since he couldn't coordinate the muscles properly, he was holding everything in until an accident happened. This often happened at the most inconvenient times like while driving or in a restaurant. There were so many challenges we faced at that time including Elliott's allergic reactions to peanuts and bee stings. He was also asthmatic and ended up in the emergency department many times in the middle of the night.

While I was recovering from my thyroid surgery, I was grateful to have help at home from the ABA services. They taught Elliott the pre-requisite of learning, including how to attend to tasks, follow instructions, and express himself with words and eventually sentences. They taught him how to play different board games in preparing him to play with other kids. They also taught him how to climb on play structures, go up and down the stairs, how to put on clothes, coordinate colors of tops and pants, and to bring plates to the sink after meals. These are easy tasks for 3-4 years old children, but they weren't easy for Elliott, who was 6-7 years old at the time. The ABA therapists were truly sent by God and were very patient, kind and positive. They worked wonders by providing Elliott with consistent, structured programs, paired with positive reinforcement in order to achieve measurable results.

Besides these basic skills, the ABA therapists had helped Elliott in many other areas. Due to his hypersensitivity to touch and the sound of the clipper, getting a haircut was tremendously difficult for Elliott. He was also afraid that the hairdresser might cut his head. So we couldn't take him to the barber or he would end up on the floor struggling to get away. It was always an embarrassing scene for us to have to explain to others why he was behaving the way he did. With the ABA program, he was able to gradually overcome the fear of these sounds and the touch of the clipper. One therapist even let him cut her beautiful, long, curly hair in exchange for allowing her to cut his hair. Eventually, I was able to cut his hair at home and now even at the barber.

Another major hurdle was to get his blood drawn for tests and to get a shot. Again, because of his hypersensitivity to touch and the fear of pain, he wouldn't stay still in order to allow the nurse to draw blood or give him an injection. He would try to run away or he wouldn't let us get close to him because he knew we would hold him firmly in order to stabilize his arm for the blood draw or injection. Often we would both end up on the floor struggling. My heart would be pounding and my arms would be exhausted from the fight of holding him down. He would be crying and everyone in the waiting room of the clinic would be looking at us. In those situations, I learned to ignore what other people might think of Elliott and I. Most people didn't understand what we had to go through in the simplest situations, as Elliott didn't have any obvious external deficit.

With the help of an amazing ABA therapist, I would take pictures of the hospital clinic to prepare him ahead of time. The therapist then set up a home program using step-by-step picture instructions to prepare Elliott for the next blood draw or injection. She would coordinate with the hospital lab to allow him to come for a trial practice or pretend blood draw. She brought him to the hospital to practice every week until he was ready. Then she coached him through the actual blood draw to make sure the experience was successful. This was the technique we used to prepare Elliott for every new experience, including waiting in line at the store, deciding what to do on a Saturday or any holiday, waiting in line at the amusement park, taking a ride on the train or BART, going through the security check point at the airport, surviving a long road trip and a dental visit. Everything in our life had to be broken down into small steps and slow motion in order to give Elliott time to prepare both mentally and emotionally.

Dropping Elliott off at a babysitter was out of the question, as he would not go with anyone except Derrick or me. We didn't go out on dates for the first 15 years of our marriage. In order to survive, we would take turns having breaks or quiet time in order to be refreshed. We had to be very creative and treasured the moments we had together to talk and share our hearts after Elliott had gone to bed. It was not always easy. If it weren't for the grace of God, our family would probably have fallen apart. I never stopped counting His blessings and His goodness towards us, which were seen each and every day.

Often, I pondered about how God took us from Canada to California, even before we knew about Elliott's diagnosis. He prepared our path and every step. He saw the bigger picture before we did. He was always there to guide us through every step.

Through it all, our "spiritual muscles" and character was being developed during the most difficult times.

Chapter 6

The Darkness Before Dawn

With the help of the ABA aide in the mainstream classroom, Elliott was doing very well in kindergarten. His teacher was very supportive and allowed the aide to facilitate Elliott's learning and participation in class. He was happy, although he still couldn't make friends and had no interest to do so.

Other parents in the class noticed Elliott's issues and were tolerant, but they never invited him for play dates or birthday parties, even though I tried very hard to invite them. I realized that I couldn't expect everyone to like Elliott or understand what he was going through. From then on, I made a point to let Elliott know how much he was loved by his parents and his Father God in Heaven. We reminded Elliott that God created him and loved him unconditionally, and that he was very special. I wanted to prepare him for the cruelty of others and rejection he might receive in the real world. By knowing that he is loved and secure, the cruelty and rejection of the real world would not even matter because he would have a healthy self image.

When Elliott entered first grade, I initially thought everything was fine as he continued to have an ABA aide in the mainstream classroom. But one day in February 2006, after Elliott had finished his writing homework, he suddenly crumbled up his paper in frustration. I asked him why he had done so, and he told me, through tears, that his teacher wouldn't like his handwriting. Where did this feeling come from? I had never heard Elliott express how he felt before, at least not in a full sentence. For him to burst out like that, I knew he must have gotten a lot of pressure from his teacher. In my heart, I could feel his hurt, discouragement and anger, but I wouldn't allow him to feel negatively about himself. I immediately pulled him into my arms and hugged him in order to comfort him. I took that opportunity to tell him how much he was loved and that he was doing a great job in writing his sentences. Then, I walked him through a prayer of forgiveness towards his teacher for making him feel frustrated and for hurting his heart.

This turned into an opportunity to explain to him how much Jesus loved him, and that He died on the cross so that we didn't have to bear the consequences of our sin. I then asked Elliott if he wanted to ask Jesus into His heart and let Him heal his hurt. Elliott said yes! I led him in a prayer to invite Jesus into his heart as his Savior and Lord. He felt better. It was a very special day for Elliott and me, as God turned a negative moment into an opportunity to lead Elliott into salvation and a personal connection with Jesus.

I remember the day when I prayed the same prayer to receive Jesus in my heart at 19 years old. It was like a sudden peace that came upon me and I felt everything was going to be all right. Elliott was 8 years old. Though he was unable to tell me how he felt, his countenance showed that his frustration and sadness were gone.

Meanwhile, as a mom, my protective instinct caused me to seek out the truth of what Elliott was going through in the classroom. I found out from the ABA aide the next day that Elliott was being sent outside the classroom whenever the teacher heard him speaking loudly. The teacher probably felt he was distracting the class by speaking loudly. I knew teachers in general education classrooms might not have much training in handling autistic kids. So I called an IEP meeting in order to request a transfer to a more supportive classroom with a special education teacher that would accommodate his needs. My intent was not to break up a good and respectful relationship with the school district, but to find a classroom where he could learn and thrive.

It turned out that the school district would not allow children to be transferred at the end of the school year, so I could only make a request and plan for the next school year. I held back my emotion, counting down the weeks before the end of the school year, while watching his behavior deteriorate every day. He would scream out loud in order to get out of the classroom. He learned that if he couldn't get a positive response or attention from others for doing good, he could scream and cause everyone to react in anger. Then they would send him out of the classroom. He would kick, throw things and hit the classroom aide. The aide was so fed up that she resigned and the ABA company described Elliott as "aggressive and hurting others every day". In order to protect their staff from injury, they sent in a different aide each day. The change of faces every day and the inconsistency of approaches was extremely stressful for Elliott. My heart hurt when I came to pick him up each day and found out about his negative behavior and how it was being handled. To protect my heart, I had to numb my emotions and "thicken my skin", and just wished the school year would end swiftly.

At the same time, I was imagining how helpless Elliott felt when he went to school each day. He couldn't express himself well enough with words, or even understand the different kinds of emotions he was experiencing. He was probably suppressing his feelings until he couldn't hold them in any longer, and then he would burst out into "aggressive behavior". I once heard it said: "behavior *is* a way of communication." That would imply if one were willing to find out what caused the behavior and not just react to the behavior, a child could be better helped to act appropriately.

Every day after school, I played the part of a detective in order to find out the reason for Elliott's negative behavior. I continued to love him, hug him and participate in all the therapies that he attended, such as

ABA, speech and occupational therapy in order to try to find ways to help him grow. I even took classes on some of the sound techniques, such as therapeutic listening and interactive metronome, and invested in equipment that helped his development in sensory processing, focus, attention and language. Elliott was making gradual, though slow, improvement in his language development, and he appeared to process information quicker than before.

The following school year (second grade), he returned to the special education classroom with an ABA aide and a very supportive special education teacher. My goal was for Elliott to recover from the emotional stress he experienced in the mainstream classroom, though his behavior was still fluctuating.

Elliott took the bus to school every day. I had him listen to therapeutic music while he was getting on the bus in order to keep him calm. However, the teacher said he was often very anxious when he arrived at school. He would ask repetitive questions and demanded them to be answered right away. I later found out that all of his repetitive questions were caused by stress, as the bus driver sometimes took different routes. Elliott was so sensitive to any slight change in his routine causing him a lot of stress. A bus ride to school might be fun for some kids, but not for Elliott. It was the cause of stress and anxiety every morning.

At the end of third grade, Elliott had to take the Star Test, which was required for all school students in

California. This was his first paper and pencil test. Since he was very behind in English, he was stressed about it and threw a temper tantrum, pushing his table away. I thought that was the end of his academic career because all school children were required to take the test. That year, the school psychologist had to do a triennial evaluation of Elliott to make sure he still qualified for the special education program due to autism. Because of his delay in multiple areas, especially in language development, the tests labeled him with severe mental retardation. Even so, the school psychologist knew he could do better because deep in her heart and through her own observation, she saw strength in him. Therefore she did all she could to advocate for him to receive all of the services he needed throughout the summer, including occupational therapy, speech therapy, and ABA services.

In the fall of 2008, Elliott was placed in another elementary school for 4th grade. Since he did so well in the special education program in 2nd and 3rd grade, we didn't expect any problems, even with the change of school and teacher. To my surprise, the school district took away the ABA trained aide without warning and provided an aide that didn't know Elliott. She didn't understand that Elliott needed positive encouragement in order to succeed. She would often use her own way to make him conform, yet without the ABA trained aide, it didn't take much time before problems occurred.

Even though Elliott's aide had been working in that school for a long time, she had never worked with a child as spirited as Elliott. She often ignored his questions, but didn't realize that by doing so, he would find other ways, often negative, to get the attention he needed. She didn't understand that in the mind of an autistic child, there were millions of questions in the brain that were looking for answers, and yet he didn't have the ability to filter them. This affected Elliott's ability to focus on what the teacher was teaching. The ABA consultant continued to come to the classroom to provide strategies in order to help Elliott participate in class.

For some reason, the teacher and the aide were not able to follow through with the recommendation of the ABA consultant. Despite their efforts, Elliott's behavior started to deteriorate. This negative behavior included making high pitch noises in class, eloping when making trips to the bathroom, pushing the screen buttons at the school gym and watching the screen drop, and turning the computer on and off. The most disturbing situation was that he would run into other classrooms and interrupt other teachers, and then stand there and laugh.

His teacher and aide were upset about his behavior, so Elliott was given a time out. He was told to write pages of negative sentences as consequences such as: "I will stop laughing when told" and "I will not use the printer." Elliott was making everyone upset instead of learning academics. There was a time when he was screaming so loudly that the entire class would have to vacate the classroom. The classroom was literally turned into a zoo, so chaotic and out of order. At one point, his aide got a bruised eye when Elliott's elbow hit her as she tried to hold him back and he resisted.

Every day I would receive a note or phone call from the teacher or the principal as to how disruptive he was in school. Even with the help of the ABA consultant giving the aide and teacher input and recommendations, they still couldn't turn the situation around as the negative behavior had gone too far.

Feeling helpless and stressed, often I would cry in the middle of the night. It left me feeling angry and ashamed. In the culture I grew up in, teachers were respected and students were expected to follow order and instruction. I was expected to behave well and to speak softly in class. I was a good student and had never caused problems at school. There was expectation to teach our children well and to behave respectfully towards others, never causing trouble. No matter what I did and what the ABA consultant tried, Elliott's behavior was still unruly. I knew there were times and situations where he couldn't control himself. He was most likely under a lot of stress by everyone seeing him as a troublemaker. Nevertheless, I felt ashamed and embarrassed. I knew that the teachers and the aide were trying their best to help, but they could no longer do anything to help as things were totally out of control. The only thing I could do was to pray and hope that the school year would end soon or that Elliott's behavior would turn around.

Sadly, I found him sitting in front of the computer one morning saying to himself: "I will not listen to Kelvin, I don't have to listen to him." "Look, here is the noise maker." He was singing and clapping to some kind of a beat saying, "I have a bad day, I have a bad day."

It was funny but sad. He was fully aware of what was happening in the classroom and he was aware of what others called him. But what else could I do to help him? I lost hope. I looked inward and only saw sadness and grief. I had forgotten to look up to Jesus. Instead of having faith, I found myself having a lot of doubt. I remembered the picture God showed me when Elliott was 6 years old. The picture was that one-day he would be speaking eloquently to a crowd wearing a grey colored suit. But at this point, I was battle weary and completely exhausted by the journey. My health had also deteriorated due to ongoing stress. I was diagnosed with high blood pressure in my 40's, which was not predominant in my family genes. I could only take so much by my own strength. I was desperate. I needed divine intervention.

To top it off, in June 2008, Elliott's baby teeth had decided to come out one after the other. The sensation of wobbly teeth caused intense discomfort to Elliott's gums and he constantly screamed in pain. He would not let me look at them. I was unable to soothe him or calm him down. He wouldn't eat much unless it was something soft. I could not stand it any more. The only thing I could think of was to distract him by having Derrick take him for a swim, which calmed him down a bit. But I desperately needed help. I tried to avoid showing my frustration in front of him. So Derrick and I would take turns to take a break in caring for Elliott. I would find myself having a quiet moment at the coffee shop or browsing the shops at the mall just for a mental break. Sometimes it was a luxury to get away to do grocery shopping. Our jobs during the day were also a type of mental refuge. I felt more successful in helping my patients to get better than in helping my own son to learn.

"God, where are you in all of this? I desperately need to hear your voice and I desperately need to see your face. Would you show yourself real to me again? When will you hear my cry? When will you come and rescue me?"

Chapter 7

The Light At The End Of The Tunnel

In the search for an answer to Elliott's behavioral issues, we took him to Bethel Church in Redding, CA in the summer of 2009. It was a five-hour drive from our home. They hosted a healing room every Saturday morning and we heard that many were healed from all kinds of sickness and diseases in the name of Jesus. So we decided to take Elliott there and give it a try.

We didn't know what to expect. When we arrived, we filled out a form regarding the problems that Elliott had, including speech and language delay, reading, fine motor and gross motor delay, difficulty with changes, anxiety and grabbing my neck when stressed. Other behavioral problems included screaming, hitting and eloping just to name a few. He was not able to relate to other peers. The list went on and on.

While we were waiting for prayer, we were spending time in the Great Room where there was worship music playing. The worship music helped us to prepare our hearts to receive prayer. There were a few ladies there making prophetic collages with magazine cut outs. So I went and asked a lady if she would make one for me. The ladies would listen to God and bring a message of encouragement to whoever asked, using magazine cut outs. The picture I received described that I was on a journey with God:

"You are called to be an intercessor. God sees your heart and He loves you very much. He will give you help to set free those who are locked up. You are a house of prayer. You are to pray when it's hard. No one knows what you are going through, but God knows. Praying creatively, as you are creative, is a quiet way to advance the kingdom of God. You will be a ransom for many and bring many into the kingdom of God".

These pictures thrilled me. It reminded me of my job to intercede for Elliott and also for his friends so that they could also be set free from the prison of autism. I was greatly encouraged.

When it was our turn to receive prayer, two people were assigned to us. At that time, Elliott would not let anyone that he didn't know walk close to him or lay hands and touch him due to his hypersensitivity to touch. So the prayer team prayed for him at a distance. Then they started to lay hands on me and intercede deeply for me. Under the healing power of the Holy

Spirit, the deep wound of pain in this journey of parenthood was exposed and dug out of my heart. I cried so much and yet the deep pain in my heart was removed. The heaviness that weighed on my heart due to Elliott's behavioral problems at school was lifted off from me. The prayer team continued to pray for me and reconfirmed my calling and prophesied that God was going to use our journey to heal many others. In my mind, the picture of Elliott wearing a gray colored suit and speaking eloquently before a huge crowd appeared again. It was confirmed once again that God was going to heal Elliott so that he would testify and glorify Him.

On the next day at the Sunday church services, another lady from the prayer team was praying for us. She was an older lady with gray hair. She told us that she had a daughter with brain damage who was 25 years old and she had been raising her just like her other children. That encouraged me and changed my attitude towards Elliott. I had decided to take him around to places just like raising a regular child and not to be weary of how other people responded. I was reminded that Elliott was "fearfully and wonderfully made." (Ps 139:14) God also reminded me of this verse:

"Behold, children are a heritage from the Lord, the fruit of the womb is a reward. Like arrows in the hand of a warrior, so are the children of one's youth. Happy is the man who has his quiver full of them." (Ps 127: 3-5)

Elliott is the only arrow in my quiver and he is designed to hit a target that no one else can. There is a plan and a purpose for his life, but I had failed to embrace Elliott as my arrow. So I confessed to God and thanked Him for His grace, His provision, and this reminder.

This trip to Bethel Church, Redding shifted my mindset and changed my course from hopelessness to hopefulness; from sadness to joy; from strife to peace; from asking endless questions to having a sense of direction. This was probably God's way of answering my cry. Now I knew I was supposed to intercede for Elliott, to pray and lay my hands on him and pray for healing and declare his destiny. The prophetic picture He gave me was a visual cue for me to pray for Elliott's divine destiny so that I would not be distracted. I came away with renewed hope as the sense of hopelessness was broken off. I didn't realize how much pain I had piled up inside of me over the years and I was very dry physically, emotionally and spiritually. There was no life inside of me until that day. The compassion and love of God had moved the gigantic rock in my heart, and He refreshed me with the peace and joy of the Holy Spirit. I was very thankful to have this opportunity to experience God's goodness and His loving kindness.

Even though there was not much obvious change in Elliott's condition, I left that church in Redding hopeful and renewed. I realized that as a mom of a special needs child, if I didn't have peace, love and joy in my heart, I wouldn't be able to have anything to give or impart to my child. Once again I realized that I needed to take care of myself, especially spiritually, which affected my entire well-being. If I was refreshed by God I would be in a better position to deal with my work, the school, and the never-ending needs of Elliott's condition. Even though Elliott was not instantly healed from autism, I knew God had already begun the healing process. We noticed that right after that visit, he was able to speak and express himself a bit better. One morning he woke up and asked, "Where is God?". And then he answered himself and said, "God is in my heart." He recognized that he had accepted Jesus in his heart already. Derrick also heard Elliott saying a couple of sentences for the first time. We were totally amazed, giving thanks to God.

In the journey of raising Elliott, challenges are still a daily occurrence. But since visiting Bethel Church in Redding, I started to seek after God for every challenge that I faced because He promised to be with me. If I lacked wisdom or solutions, I could always talk to God and ask Him to help.

In July 2009, Elliott needed to get a vaccine and he was extremely afraid of needles. Besides the actual poke of the needle, which really didn't hurt a lot; the perception of pain, the anticipation and the fear of the situation just made him freeze and scared and stopped him from living a free life. He would get up in the morning and ask me, "Is it the day for the vaccine?" He would cry, holding me tight or pace around without having the appetite for breakfast. He was getting more and more anxious after preloading him with a visual schedule and coaching. I was asking God how I could help him to be calm enough to 'survive' the needle injection. God gave me a Bible verse that said:

"...casting all your care upon Him, for He cares for you." (I Peter 5:7)

How could I explain to Elliott how to "cast" and how it was related to his fear and anxiety? So He gave me a picture of a paper basket, and the fear and anxiety was symbolically written on a piece of paper. I then crunched the paper into a paper ball and threw it into the paper basket. In doing so, he was throwing away the piece of paper with the fear and anxiety without taking it back. So I demonstrated to Elliott how it could be done and he practiced. Sure enough he grasped the concept quickly as this strategy was simple and given by God who knows him well. After throwing two paper balls into the basket, he was able to settle down and not be distracted by the thought of the vaccine. He was then able to go on with his day. On the day of the vaccine, he casted the paper balls again twice to help his fear. While he was waiting for the injection in the waiting room, he asked for prayer and the injection went smoothly with the help of the ABA therapists. It was a great success over all.

It is important for me to continue to walk this journey by cultivating a closer relationship with God. I read the Bible, meditate on His Words, talk to Him daily and quietly listen to His instructions. Sometimes I would hide away in a quiet corner at a coffee shop while waiting for Elliott to finish his therapy. I would pray and talk to God, telling Him how I felt and what was on my mind. I also asked God what was on His mind. I have grown to be a friend of God as He promised to lead me and guide me on this path.

"He leads me in the paths of righteousness." (Psalm 23:3)

Ever since the trip to Bethel Church, deep healing occurred through the prayers. I was able to let go and trust God more knowing that He really is the One who protects and helps Elliott to grow. With this new revelation of how precious God sees Elliott, I started to take him out more often and try many different activities just like an ordinary family would. We took him to the beach, even though the sound of waves might be overwhelming for him. He might be running away from the wave and stayed far away from the water. At least we got him exposed to different experiences and we challenged him to adjust and overcome.

Derrick and I started to do things together with Elliott and we had a lot of fun. We joined special needs programs that were available for families with autistic children, such as kayaking and boogie boarding with the help of many volunteers. The first time was very challenging as he wouldn't get in the kayak and he would just pace along the beach pinching me because of his fear and stress. Then at the end, he would agree to get in the kayak only if he could sit on Derrick's lap. When we heard the cheers of all the volunteers and their smiles on their faces for just the tiny step he took, my tears flowed. How good is our Lord!! He put so many people along our path to cheer us on!! Even though Elliott would cry as he couldn't regulate his excitement and the sound of the loud cheers, our hearts melted by such love! This was a major breakthrough in our family life. Once again we dared to step out to try new things. With this new hope and faith in God, it was clear that He is my sure help in time of trouble.

> "The salvation of the righteous is from The Lord, He is their strength in the time of trouble." (Ps. 37:39)

Chapter 8

My Journey With God

When Elliott turned 12 in March 2010, he desired to spend his birthday weekend at Bethel Church again instead of having a birthday party. So we went. While we were waiting for prayer in the Great Room, the Holy Spirit began to whisper to me:

> "Helen, nothing is impossible for Me, and nothing is too big for Me. Helen, I love you, and I love Elliott. Helen, I love you. Just believe for the impossible, for nothing is impossible for Me. I will open your eyes to see what is impossible for man but is possible for Me. Helen, don't think upon the little things, for I have called you, Elliott and Derrick for impossible things. Therefore trust in Me, rest in Me."

> "Helen, change is coming, change for the good and for the better. There will be change in Elliott's situation and there will be change in Derrick 's Job.

Don't be alarmed for I am at work for my children. Helen, trust in Me and prophesy over your life and your family's destiny. I who have begun the good work will certainly finish it. I am not a God of little ability. I can create mountains and seas. I parted the Red Sea and rescued My people. I can certainly save My children who seek after Me and desire to do My work. Helen, you are called to the highest. You will see angels and many kings. You are to go to the nations to minister with great anointing and see signs and wonders that is why I have given you a foretaste of what is to come. Remember those days and what I deposited in you in Hawaii, Finland, Argentina, Peru and in every circumstance. They were all to show you My presence in every single situation. There might have been times where I seemed far away but it was because you didn't sought Me out but instead just ran round and round with your own strength. But in fact, you surely can find me. Just seek Me. The best is yet to come."

I was so touched by God's assurance of His help and His presence. I knew He was onto something and my job was just to trust and obey Him.

Then it was our turn to get prayer. Again Elliott would not let anyone touch him due to his hypersensitivity. So the prayer team began to pray for me. I felt God was saying to me, "I have not forgotten about you. I have given you the anointing for breakthrough." I asked God for a picture of what that would look like. Then I saw a picture of Elliott going with me everywhere testifying of God's goodness.

Then one of the prayer team members gave me a picture. He said he saw me like in the time of Noah as the land was covered by lots of water for a long time during the big flood. The flood wiped out all mankind because of their sin. Noah heard God and built a huge boat and he went in the boat with his family and animals before the flood started. So he was saved during the flood. Then the time came when the floodwaters receded and he sent out the dove to test if there was life and dry land. The dove then came back with a freshly plucked olive leaf signifying that the flooded water had receded and there was life outside the boat. (Genesis 6-8)

The prayer team member said it was the time of new beginnings for Elliott and me. Even the journey was like a flood, so overwhelming but it was the time of new beginning and new covenant. I asked God, "What does it look like outside the ark?" I felt God was saying, "It's bright and new and there are no boundaries, but it was to be experienced and guided by Me." The prayer team member went on to say that he felt Elliott had such a smart mind that he could overcome his difficulty by shifting his mindset and he continued to pray for peace for Elliott.

Again, this prayer and encounter with God was not something I took lightly. And even more stunning was that the prophetic art lady in the Great Room made a collage for Elliott. The collage was a picture of a golden station wagon driving around a mountain as if having some kind of outdoor adventures. She described that Elliott would have some kind of ministry that would have a world-class destination. He would be armed with imagination, living at the right hand of Christ, as he is precious to Jesus. When he thinks he cannot do it, he will remember that God said he could.

The road would never be the same again. This trip to Bethel Church again brought both Elliott and me another step forward in faith, confirming God's plan for Elliott. He also assured me of His presence and guidance on our journey. In June 2010, Elliott graduated from 5th grade and he walked down the aisle with his classmates wearing a suit. My tears fell and my heart rejoiced in God's goodness in taking him so far.

At that time, he still had a lot of challenges with reading comprehension, stress and anxiety with change, and he had no interest in making friends with his peers. Even with the little improvement in speech that we saw, our hearts were filled with hope because of the prophetic destiny God showed me in the last two trips to the healing rooms at Bethel Church. God has so much grace that He would give me these pictures to encourage me so that I would not be discouraged when things are difficult at times and when I am totally overwhelmed and tired. This is His promise to His people:

"The Lord will give strength to His people; The Lord will bless His people with peace." (Ps. 29:11)

After the summer, Elliott was excited to start middle school at our neighborhood school. He was prepared with a nice haircut and a new backpack. With excitement and anticipation, I took him to school on the first day of 6th grade in September 2010.

The school campus was full of students. The noise level was overwhelming even for me. But we were eagerly waiting to meet the teacher and also the one-on-one aide assigned to Elliott. It was part of our IEP contract that Elliott would have an ABA trained aide to assist him. So I waited and waited and there was no one. An hour into the first session, there was no aide in sight. I was told by the teacher to talk to the principal, so I did. She didn't know anything about it. She was very apologetic and was trying to contact the School District to find someone for him. I was afraid that history would repeat itself like in the elementary school years. Therefore I felt I needed to make sure Elliott 's need for proper support in class was followed through.

The next day, an aide came to the classroom. It didn't take long to find out that she didn't know how to handle Elliott's behavior, as she didn't have ABA training. She ended up getting into power struggles with him. Elliott needed a lot of positive encouragement to learn rather than punishment. Punishment only caused more fear, stress and anxiety, which perpetuated even more negative behavior in him. He would elope, scream, hit, and run into the girls' bathroom to get adult attention. On the other hand, he strived for positive encouragement, which gave him confidence and encouraged him to do what was right and appropriate. It was quite clear that Elliott resorted to negative behavior when facing a change of school, a change of teacher and environment.

Within one month after school began, he was suspended for 10 days for hitting others and running into the girls' bathroom. Again, my heart sank every time I received a phone call at work from the school that I needed to take him home because he was hitting. This caused a lot of interruptions in my work schedule, as I would have to cancel all of my patient appointments with short notice and I could never predict what would happen the next day. From being filled with hope to having to deal with the extreme behavioral issues, I didn't know what to do except to hold onto the prophetic picture I received for Elliott and to declare it daily in my prayers. We knew this was a critical moment to support Elliott and find ways to help him.

We decided to call a meeting with the School District and advocate for an ABA trained aide who would use positive behavior management techniques to help him. Honestly, I was a bit fearful because I didn't want to ruin the relationship with the school. We wanted to work with the school to get Elliott the help he needed.

Continuing to seek God, I prayed, asking Him for direction and strategies as to how I should handle the meeting. I felt that He was giving me a picture of the meeting room where Jesus was sitting there with me, and there were two angels in the corner of the room. I knew if God was with me in this meeting, then I would win. If He was not in it, then I'd better not do anything because I knew I would not win.

> "For we do not wrestle against flesh and blood, but against principalities, powers, against the rulers of the darkness of this age, against spiritual hosts of wickedness in the heavenly places." (Ephesians 6:12)

On the day of the meeting, we found out that a high-ranking school administrator would be attending the meeting. I was worried and full of fear. I suddenly remembered to stop looking at the fear and intimidation that could easily come upon me, but instead I looked to Jesus and asked Him, "Lord, are you there with me? I won't go in unless you are there with me." Then I sensed His presence and I saw two angels at the corner of the meeting room. That reassurance was all I needed. So I boldly presented my case in front of the school administrator and she approved a trial period of one month with an ABA aide for Elliott, who was then allowed to return to school. I was very thankful for God's faithfulness in keeping His promises.

Interestingly enough, as soon as the ABA aide came, Elliott's behavioral issues were instantly resolved. There was no more eloping, hitting, screaming or running into the girls' bathroom for attention seeking, and he was settling down to learn in class. In the subsequent meeting with the school administrator, she had no reason for not continuing the ABA aide for Elliott and so he was having a very good school year while excelling in mathematics in his special education classroom. All I can say is that the battle belongs to the Lord and He will fight for His children.

We continued to bring him to the Bethel Church's healing rooms for prayer whenever we could, especially on his birthday (per his request) and during Thanksgiving weekend at the end of November. We believed ever since the first time we visited the healing room in 2009 that the healing process had begun in Elliott. As we held onto the slightest improvement and gave thanks to God, our faith rose up and we believed for more because we knew God was able and willing to do it again.

On his birthday weekend in March 2011, we were again at Bethel Church's healing rooms. A lady at the prophetic art table was drawing a picture for Elliott. When I looked at the stick figure drawing in front of me, I could not stop crying. The lady wondered what was going on and was curious to hear my perception of the picture. When I was able to control my tears, I told her the picture she drew was exactly like the one God gave me when Elliott was 6 years old. That was the time when he had just been diagnosed with autism. The stick figure picture illustrated him speaking to a crowd, and that he was going to be very good at computers or learning a lot about computers. It also depicted that he was very smart and intelligent, full of compassion with a gentle spirit. He was also enjoying life and he would be part of the business and market place mountain, teaching a lot of people. I couldn't believe my eyes! I couldn't believe how much God loved us and especially Elliott!

He has a special calling on Elliott's life and even when I forgot about the picture that He gave me in 2004, or when I was disillusioned and tired, God has never forgotten what He has created Elliott for. His plan and intent for him has never changed. God reminded us that we have not missed a step no matter how much hardship we incurred or how many detours there seems to be on the journey of pursuing the fulfillment of our destiny. God is faithful and wastes no time. Every step in the journey we took, God was using it to prepare us for our destiny.

Chapter 9

I Can Dream Again

Seven years after Elliott was formally diagnosed with autism, he decided to publicly acknowledge Jesus Christ as his Lord and Savior by being water baptized on June 26, 2011. Pastor Greg Simas, at Convergence House of Prayer, baptized him. It was the most cheerful and happy baptism as everyone at church rejoiced with us. Besides the healing prayers received in the healing room at Bethel Church in Redding, a supportive and loving church community is key to our journey in raising Elliott.

Elliott used to talk so loudly during quiet prayer meetings at church which made me worry that he would disturb the pastor during church service. But pastor Wendi Simas said that it was no problem and this helped her to focus better. The shame, guilt and rejection that I anticipated just as I received from my friends was all lifted off from my shoulders. There were many times when Elliott would talk loudly or laugh in the middle of the sermon, and our pastor would say, "Oh,

Elliott agrees with what I said". He never gave him a disapproving look or gestured for someone to remove him from the service. There was such grace, love and kindness demonstrated. We also have many adult church friends that don't mind Elliott coming along for lunch after church and some really enjoy interacting with him, even if he asks them silly questions repeatedly such as, "Do you know who is Joe Blow?" "Have you taken the mono vaccine?" New people in the church would often say to me, "Your son has such a nice smile."

During Thanksgiving weekend in November 2011, we went to Bethel Church again hoping to receive another level of healing for Elliott. I vividly remember that Friday evening service. The speaker had just returned from New Zealand. He reported with excitement that a child with autism was completely healed in New Zealand after being prayed for over a few years. The doctors even gave him a clean bill of health. The whole church was excited about the good news and I knew immediately that God was going to do something special during this trip for Elliott, and that we were not here by accident. The speaker not only gave thanks to God for the healing testimony, he also went after the condition by asking everyone who had families or knew someone that had autism to stand up. Then he asked those that had a heart to see autism healed to stand up. They stood and prayed for those families and children. Once again my eyes were soaked with tears. How great is our God! He knew why we were there. He saw my heart and the burden I carried as a mom and He motivated people to pray for us and many other families that had been locked up in the autism jail cell. He desires to set us all free!!

I felt The Lord was whispering to me, "Won't you believe I will heal him completely? I care about him so much that I have the whole church praying for him! I will complete the work that I have started. I will do it. It is complete." At the healing room the next morning, Elliott asked for very specific prayer in different areas where he felt he needed prayer. He saw previous prayers being answered and he came in with faith. The prayer team submitted the prayers to God knowing He knew exactly what Elliott needed. The prayer team went on to prophesy over him saying "he would be instrumental in making changes in the educational system. He might not necessarily be a teacher, but he would stand in front of people speaking, writing books and impacting the nations."

I was so overwhelmed by the healing prayer and the prophetic words that were released. It seemed as if God was showing me a little more each time of Elliott's prophetic destiny. As a mom, I take note of every word spoken over him and continue to pray for him according to God's intention. This is a journey of partnership with God to release *the arrow in my quiver* for the target he is designed to hit.

There is no doubt that God has been gracious to me as He allows me to see glimpses of what Elliott 's future would look like so that when I come across difficult situations, I would not get discouraged. In April 2012 Elliott again had a difficult time at school due to the stress and anxiety associated with staff changes in school and his behavior deteriorated again. My heart was hurting so much for him as I thought about what he had to go through each day. I again held onto the promises that were given to him, declaring them while I was working with the school to come up with a solution. It would have been very easy to look at the difficult situation and get discouraged and let doubt come into my mind. However, because His promises said,

"If God is for us, who can be against us?" (Romans 8:31)

I learned to turn away from the facts of the situation and choose to believe in the truth. The truth is:

"He was wounded for our transgressions; He was bruised for our iniquities; the chastisement for our peace was upon Him, and by His stripes we are healed." (Isaiah 53:5)

"Being confident of this very thing, that He who has began a good work in you will complete it until the day of Jesus Christ." (Philippians 1:6)

"And my God shall supply all your need according to His riches in glory in Christ Jesus." (Philippians 4:19)

"Now to Him who is able to do exceedingly abundantly above all that we ask or think,

according to the power at work within us."
(Ephesians 3:20)

"... Which is Christ in you, the hope of glory."
(Colossians 1:27)

So I declared these Bible truths over Elliott and I saw his face light up as his spirit agreed with what God said about him.

When Elliott was stressed out about changes or unknown situations, I would help him to understand and find solutions. I explained to him what God recommended us to do through the Bible:

"Do not be anxious about anything, but in everything by prayer and supplication with thanksgiving let your requests be made known to God. And the peace of God, which surpassed all understanding, will guard your hearts and your minds in Christ Jesus." (Phil 4:6-7 ESV)

He would then feel better. The Word of God became his solution to many problems and I would pray for him using the truth of the Bible.

In this journey of raising Elliott, I learned to use positive and encouraging words in building Elliott 's confidence and self-esteem. By declaring God's promises and prophetic pictures over him, I am agreeing with God in partnership with Him in molding Elliott into the person God intended him to be. I am not alone in this journey. I can trust God to keep His promises. I can dream again and be full of hope.

By the time this book is published, we have taken Elliott to Bethel Church 14 times, and we have witnessed improvement by leaps and bounds. Many areas of difficulty have disappeared. He has become more coordinated in swimming which allowed him to participate in the high school swim team and snorkel in the ocean during our family vacation. He used to have no interest in making friends and he was only comfortable with adults. He is now "Mr. Social" and he intentionally talks to other high school teenagers, the cashier at the check out line and initiates a conversation with young people in the youth group at church. He also hangs out with friends or calls them by phone. He no longer gets frustrated while waiting for an airplane to take off. He can sit back and relax on the plane while checking out all the actions of the ground crew and he looks forward to the next plane trip.

He is now able to sit calmly in the dentist chair for his cleaning and he successfully completed one year of wearing corrective braces. His strength is in mathematics and he was able to study Algebra with other regular children in high school. The reading expert at a reputable reading program reported that although his reading level was behind, his mathematics was at the 12th grade level when he was in the 9th grade. He is now able to sit through 4 hours of the reading program with a few breaks and minimal behavioral issues, which are significant improvements compared to one year ago.

There is no more hitting, eloping or screaming at school. He is very motivated to achieve well and he does not settle for a 'B' on his report card. He works hard for an 'A' in all his subjects. He is also very adventurous and good with directions. He is always our GPS when we miss an exit on the highway. He volunteered at the local food bank sorting and packing bags of donated food. He connects with God by hearing and seeing what He wants to say to him that day. Just this summer, Derrick started to teach him computer programming and the list just goes on.

As I look back, I cannot stop giving thanks to my Lord God. His love and His goodness endure forever!! There are many challenges in raising a son with autism. But I will look beyond the pain, stress, shame, fear, hopelessness and despair and count on the promises of God as He promises to be with me. I am not alone on this journey. I can see the light at the end of the tunnel.

My prayer is that my journey would encourage you. I know each child with autism might present a different set of challenges. Your story and your circumstances might be different from mine. You might still feel overwhelmed and confused or even feel angry. But just remember you are not alone. God loves you and cares very much for you and your child. He has made you and your child for a special purpose. In the book of John (John 9:1-3), there was a man blind from birth. Jesus' disciples asked Him, "Rabbi, who sinned, this man or his parents, that he was born blind?" Jesus answered, "Neither this man nor his parents sinned but that the works of God should be revealed in him."

I can testify how true this is in Elliott 's situation. God has given Elliott a special set of gifts and talents that is designed for a special target. I would not have been able to discover that if I didn't turn around and look to God for the solution. There are many treatments or therapies available for autism. Some are experimental and some cost a lot of time and financial resources. Some work for one family but not the other. The wisdom in discerning what is the best for your child at certain ages or stages is beyond common sense. I believe that God has given us a special gift in that He wants to show us how to 'decode' the gift box so that we can discover the treasure inside our child. He is waiting for you to know Him and connect with Him. He will carry you on this journey of raising your child with autism.

You could simply start with a prayer like this:

> "Heavenly Father, thank you for loving me and my child. Please forgive me for doing things my own way. I acknowledge that I need your help. Please come into my heart and show me your plan and your vision for my child. Give me your strength, your grace, your patience and your wisdom for raising my child to fulfill his/her calling and destiny. Thank you, Jesus, for what you did on the cross. Please send me the Holy Spirit (the Helper) to guide me through this journey, in Jesus' Name, Amen."

Footnotes

1) Murkoff, Heidi (1989) What to expect the first year (Pocket book)

2) Sears, Martha and William MD (1997) Complete book of Christian Parenting and child care: a medical and moral guide to raising healthy children (Broadman and Holman publishers)

3) WebMD (2014) "What is attachment parenting?", Article.

4) Klein, Stanley D., PhD, Schive, Kim (2001) You will dream new dreams: inspiring personal stories by parents of children with disability (Kensington books)

About Helen M. Koon

Helen and her husband Derrick Koon are both Chinese who were born in Hong Kong and immigrated to Canada as young professionals. Helen is an occupational therapist and Derrick is a computer software engineer. They met and married in Toronto, Canada in 1994 and their son Elliott was born in 1998 before they moved to Foster City (30 min. south of San Francisco, California, USA). They are both Christians and they intend to raise their son in a warm Christian home. The arrival of Elliott has completely changed their lives. While they both desire to transform their workplace by bringing the presence of God in their scope of influence, creating software and touching people's lives, Helen is also passionate about going to the nations and setting the captives free and healing the broken hearted. They have lived and worked in many different countries and enjoy traveling.

Helen can be contacted on Facebook at:
https://www.facebook.com/anarrowinmyquiver

www.ingramcontent.com/pod-product-compliance
Lightning Source LLC
LaVergne TN
LVHW021611080426
835510LV00019B/2517